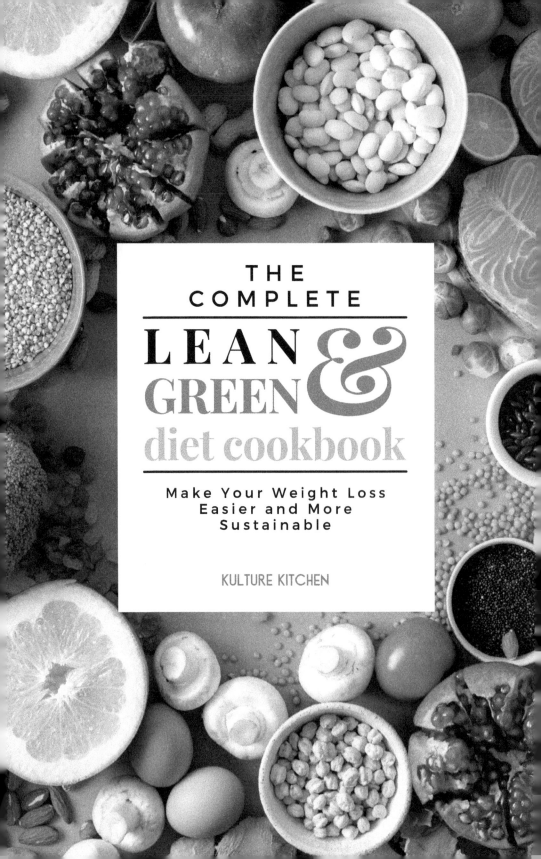

THE COMPLETE

LEAN & GREEN

diet cookbook

Make Your Weight Loss Easier and More Sustainable

KULTURE KITCHEN

KULTURE
KITCHEN

PUBLISHING HOUSE

www.kulturekitchenpublishing.com

Recipes by Audrey Chambers

Photography: Humbert Castillo

Graphic design: Tori Vergara

Editorial coordination: Joe Garcia and Humbert Castillo

First edition March 2021

KULTURE
KITCHEN

PUBLISHING HOUSE

THE COMPLETE

LEAN

GREEN

DIET COOKBOOK

The Power of Fueling Hacks Meals 2 in 1

Audrey Chambers

CONTENTS

Audrey Chambers

Audrey Chambers is a passionate cookbook writer with a decade of professional culinary expertise. Known for her culinary skills and high standard, she has combined her classic recipes tailored to use with the modern cooking appliance in her new cookbook series "The Complete Lean & Green Diet Cookbook" for Kulture Kitchen Publishing House. She loves to employ innovations in cooking by keeping the traditional elements and richness.

We can always find the art of simplicity in her recipes, making her a step ahead of many innovative cooking methods. All of her books include self-tested recipes, and the pleasure of sharing exciting experiments is evident in most of her recipe works.

Popularly known as a "recipe development whiz" among her circle, she contributes recipes to several reputed magazines. She helps you discover something new and impressive. Beyond her books, she maintains a strong influence among her friends and family as an enthusiast of healthy eating and living.

Having spent considerable time writing the series "The Complete Lean & Green Diet Cookbook" she has carefully penned her research with super versatile meal ideas without compromising quality and nutritional values. Her approach to modern food tech is mind-blowing. This Cookbook Series is a pioneering endeavor blended with modern cooking with traditional values by focusing on healthy, balanced food. It is a reference series for people who love having healthy food.

INTRODUCTION

Many people die of chronic diseases caused by unhealthy choices. Many of us are eating more than what we need. When it comes to losing weight or fat, it is best to eat meals explicitly designed for this purpose. This allows the body to receive the most benefit from a calorie-restricted diet. Lean and Green Meals were designed with this in mind and can help you lose weight and fat through simple portion-controlled meals and snacks. Studies have shown that individuals who reduce portion sizes or prioritize low-calorie density foods achieve more significant weight loss outcomes than those who follow conventional macronutrient diets.

When portion-controlled/calorie-restricted meals are employed as a lifestyle, it energizes the individual and causes them to lose weight or maintain a healthy weight. Lean and Green Meals have been successful for millions of people worldwide, allowing many people to reap the benefits of being on a weight loss regimen while keeping their food costs low.

Lose weight by eating smaller portions throughout the day. Your body will crave more food, and in turn, your metabolism will accelerate to burn as much of the food as possible. Keep in mind that exercise is also essential while following a low-calorie program. The calories you burn while working out heighten the weight loss caused by the meals. Once you get used to eating lean and green meals, your body sheds weight quickly and easily without feeling any stress. If you are looking to lose a lot of weight quickly without feeling stressed, invest in Lean and Green Meals.

Lean & Green

What is the Lean and Green Meal?

Lean and Green meals are predominantly home-cooked, high-protein, non-starchy vegetables, healthy fat, and low-calorie-efficient meals. This meal plan involves structured eating that restricts your daily caloric intake to a minimum of 1200 calories and a maximum of 1500 calories. This is significantly lower than the average daily 2000 calories required to maintain weight. The goal is to eat enough nutrients to support the body while avoiding empty, low-benefit calories. The rich meals generally consist of the following:

- High-quality protein such as eggs, chicken, turkey, pork chops, soybeans, fish, and seafood such as prawns, mussels, oysters.
- High-quality fiber foods such as oranges, peas, nuts, seeds, avocadoes, carrots, oats, apples, beets, broccoli, collard greens, swiss chard.
- High-quality vegetables such as garlic, Brussel sprouts, kale, asparagus, cucumber, spinach, ginger, cabbage.
- Good fats such as coconut oil, avocado, olive oil, etc.

Lean Meal

Lean and green meals demand that you make meals from meats. Though most weight-watchers prefer to avoid meat, it is highly nutritious. It is an excellent source of protein, vitamins, minerals, and many other food classes. To avoid it would leave a vacant spot in your diet.

Lean and Green Meals help incorporate healthy portions of high-quality lean meat into your food. The lean meats are divided into 3 categories, and you are allowed to cook from any. They include:

- Lean: comprises meat with high levels of saturated fats such as pork, lamb, sausages, salmon, and beef. These meats should be eaten in lesser quantities and without additional fat servings
- Leaner: comprises meat with moderate saturated fats such as chicken breasts, turkey, swordfish, and ground meat. Moderate ration with one healthy fat serving is allowed.
- Leanest: comprises meat with low levels of saturated fats such as cod, shrimp, prawns, game meats, egg whites. They can be consumed in high quantities with at most 2 additional healthy fat servings.

Green Meal

Also, non-starchy vegetables are categorized into (1) lower carb, (2) moderate carb, and (3) higher carb. All kinds of salad greens and green leafy vegetables have lower carbs. Moderate carb vegetables include cauliflower, and summer squash. Lastly, peppers and broccoli are high-carb vegetables.

Allowed and Avoid Foods

What to eat?
Allowed Lean and Green Meal foods include:

- Fish and Seafood: calamari, cod, shrimp, anchovies, trout, halibut, salmon, lobster tuna, crab, and scallops and shellfish, mussels, oysters, prawns
- Meat: turkey, game meats, lean beef, lamb, tenderloin or pork chop, chicken, ground beef (<85% lean)
- Eggs: egg yolks, egg whites, whisked eggs, low-fat mayonnaise
- Dairy products: low-fat or fat-free yogurt, cheese, milk, buttermilk

- Fruits: Oranges, Lemons, Limes, Avocados, Apples, Pears, Cherries, Watermelon, Cantaloupe, Peaches, Figs, Apricots, Strawberries, Blackberries, Blueberries, etc.
- Oils: canola, coconut, walnut, olive, and flaxseed oil
- Vegetables: Kale, spaghetti squash spinach, mushrooms, cucumbers, zucchini, cabbage, cauliflower, broccoli, eggplant, bell peppers, celery, jicama, Mexican potatoes
- Snacks without added sugar: popsicles, jam, chewing gum, mint.
- Goods for soy: tofu only
- Seasonings and condiments: spices, dried herbs, salt, lime juice, lemon juice, barbecue sauce, soy sauce, salsa, cocktail sauce, yellow mustard, sugar-free syrup, 1/2 teaspoon ketchup, calorie-free sweeteners, etc.

Foods to Avoid:

Most foods and beverages containing carbohydrates are prohibited when following the Lean and Green Meal lifestyle. These prohibited foods are:

- Added Sugar: Chocolate, ice cream, cotton candy, soda, candies, table sugar, sweets, pastries, energy drinks, etc.
- Refined Grains: Pasta created with refined wheat, white bread, pizza dough, etc.
- Refined oil: canola oil, soybean oil, cottonseed oil, etc.
- Drinks, etc.
- Starchy vegetables: sweet potatoes, beans, peas, white potatoes
- Trans fats: Margarine, hot dogs, deli meats, etc.
- Highly processed food

KULTURE
KITCHEN

PUBLISHING HOUSE

THE COMPLETE

LEAN

GREEN

DIET COOKBOOK

Cookbook 1
The Power of Fueling Hacks Meals
Vol. 1

Audrey Chambers

MEAT

Cajun Pork Chops and Spinach Salad

Preparation Time: 10 minutes
Cooking Time: 10–15 minutes
Servings: 4 Servings
1 Lean, 3 Greens, 3 Condiments
Ingredients:

- 8 cups baby spinach

- 28-ounce pork chops

- 1 tablespoon Cajun seasoning

- 1 cup fresh tomatoes, chopped

- 1 lemon, juiced

- 1/2 teaspoon each of salt and ground black pepper

- Lemon wedges for garnish

Directions:

1. Season the pork chops with the Cajun seasoning, 1/8 teaspoon salt, and 1/8 teaspoon pepper.

2. Set aside to marinate for about 25 minutes. (The longer, the better)Cook the pork in a preheated oven at 450 F for 10 . minutes. Meanwhile, heat the water in a pot. Attach the spinach and cook until the mixture is wilted.

3. Transfer the spinach to a bowl. Add in the tomatoes, lemon juice, the remaining salt, and pepper. Serve pork chops with spinach salad and lemon wedge(s) by the side. Enjoy!

Nutrition:

- Calories: 301;
- Carbs: 12.3g;
- Protein: 28g;
- Fat: 16g.

Classic Stuffed Bell Peppers

Preparation TIme: 10 minutes
Cooking Time: 10-15 minutes
Servings: 2
1 Lean, 3 Greens, 3 Condiments
Ingredients:

- 4 large bell peppers (any color)

- 1 pound ground deli roast beef

- 2 tablespoons chopped onions

- 1 cup shredded low- fat mozzarella cheese

- 1/4 cup low-sodium chicken broth

- 2 garlic cloves, minced

- 1 cup sliced cremini mushrooms

- 3 tablespoons reduced-fat cream cheese

Directions:

1. Preheat oven to 400° F.

2. To remove the top of the pepper, cut a thin slice from the end of each bell pepper's stem.

3. Remove the seeds and ribs, rinse the peppers, and set aside.

4. Sauté the onion and garlic in broth in a large skillet over medium-high heat until the onions are translucent, 4–5 minutes.

5. The mushrooms are added and continue to cook until tender.

6. Stir in the beef and heat through for about 4 minutes. Remove the skillet from the heat and mix in the cream cheese.

7. Line the inside of each pepper with 1/8 cup of mozzarella and an equal amount of beef mixture, and then top off with remaining cheese.

8. Bake for 18–20 minutes or until the peppers are soft and the cheese is melted.

9. Serve with bean salad for a filling lunch.

10. Enjoy!

Nutrition:
- Calories: 292;
- Protein: 32g;
- Fat: 14.7g;
- Carbs: 6.8g

Rosemary Pork

Preparation Time: 5 minutes
Cooking Time: 15-25 minutes
Servings: 4
Ingredients:

- 1 1/2 pounds thin-sliced boneless, skinless pork loin (trim out all excess fat)

- Rosemary seasoning (or garlic, rosemary, parsley, onion, black pepper, sage, thyme, salt) —1 tablespoon

- Roasted garlic oil (or garlic and oil of your choice) — 4 teaspoons

Directions:

1. Preheat your oven to 375°F.

2. Add the oil and seasoning to a bowl and mix thoroughly to combine well.

3. Pat dry the pork loin and evenly spread the seasoning on one side of the pork loin pieces.

4. Place the seasoned pork chops in a pan and put them in the oven.

5. Cook for about 25 minutes, or until the temperature of the pork gets to 150°F. Switch the pork to a plate and let it cool down for approximately 5 minutes.

Nutrition:

- Calories: 283kcal;
- Fat: 10.5g;
- Carbohydrates: 0g;
- Fiber: 0g;
- Sugar: 0g;
- Protein: 44.5g

Taco Tasty Bowls

Preparation Time: 5 minutes
Cooking Time: 15–20 minutes
Servings: 4
Ingredients:

- 1 large head Cauliflower (ready-to-cook cauliflower rice)

- 1 1/2 pound Lean ground beef

- 1-2 capfuls Southwestern seasoning (or use low-salt taco seasoning)

- 2 cups No-sugar, no-flavor added tomatoes (canned, diced)

- Favorite condiments

Directions:

1. Add the ground beef to a pan and sauté for about 12 minutes over medium-high heat or until it turns slightly brown.

2. Break the meat into smaller pieces when cooking.

3. Add the seasoning and tomatoes. Stir thoroughly.

4. Lower the heat to low and cook for extra 5 minutes, or until the liquid reduces by half.

5. Meanwhile, chop the cauliflower to make cauliflower rice.

6. Serve the cauliflower with the beef mixture, topped with condiments.

Nutrition:

- Calories: 275kcal;
- Fat: 9.9g;
- Carbohydrates: 6.2g;
- Fiber: 2.3g;
- Sugar: 3.6g;
- Protein: 39g

Beef and Broccoli

Preparation Time: 5 minutes
Cooking Time: 15 minutes
Servings: 4
Ingredients:

- 1 tablespoon Olive oil (divided)

- 1 1/2 lbs. Flank steak (thinly sliced)

- 3 Garlic cloves (minced)

- 1 Shallot (finely chopped)

- 4 Green onions (thinly sliced)

- 4 cups Broccoli florets

- 2 tablespoon Arrowroot starch

- 3/4 cup Water

- 1/3 cup Soy sauce (low-sodium)

- 2 tablespoon Coconut sugar

- 1 tsp fresh ginger (minced)

- 1/8 tsp Red pepper flakes (crushed)

Directions:

1. With your pan, heat the oil over medium-high heat.

2. Add the beef to the pan and cook until it turns brown, or about 8 minutes. Withdraw and set aside.

3. Add the garlic, green onions, and shallot to the pan.

4. Stir and cook for 1 minute.

5. Add the broccoli. Cook with the pan covered for about 5 minutes.

6. Mix the arrowroot starch and water in a bowl.

7. Add the red pepper flakes, ginger, soy sauce, and coconut sugar to a bowl and mix thoroughly.

8. Add the arrowroot mixture and combine well. Set the mixture aside.

9. Add the sauce to the pan.

10. For about 5 minutes, cook or until the sauce is slightly thick.

11. Add the beef and mix thoroughly.

12. Cook for extra 3 minutes and serve.

Nutrition:
- Calories: 306kcal;
- Fat: 13.2g;
- Carbohydrates: 19.1g;
- Fiber: 1.1g;
- Sugar: 7.7g;
- Protein: 28.9g

FISH AND SEAFOOD

Shrimp With Garlic

Preparation Time: 10 minutes
Cooking Time: 25 minutes
Servings: 2
1 Leaner, 3 Green, 1 Healthy Fat, 3 Condiments
Ingredients:

- 1 lb. shrimp

- ¼ teaspoon baking soda

- 2 tablespoons oil

- 2 teaspoon minced garlic

- ¼ cup vermouth

- 2 tablespoons unsalted butter and 1 teaspoon parsley

Directions:

1. In a bowl, toss shrimp with baking soda and salt, let it stand for a couple of minutes

2. In a skillet, heat olive oil and add shrimp

3. Add garlic, red pepper flakes and cook for 1–2 minutes

4. Add the vermouth and cook for 4–5 more minutes. When ready, remove from heat and serve

Nutrition:

- Calories: 289;
- Carbohydrate: 2 g;
- Cholesterol: 3 mg;
- Fat: 17 g;
- Fiber: 2 g;
- Protein: 7 g

Sabich Sandwich

Preparation Time: 5 minutes
Cooking Time: 15 minutes
Servings: 2
Ingredients:

- 2 tomatoes

- Olive oil

- ½ lb. eggplant

- ¼ cucumber

- 1 tablespoon lemon

- 1 tablespoon parsley

- ¼ head cabbage

- 2 tablespoons wine vinegar

- 2 pita bread

- ½ cup hummus

- ¼ tahini sauce

- 2 hard-boiled eggs

Directions:

1. In a skillet, fry eggplant slices until tender

2. In a bowl, add tomatoes, cucumber, parsley, lemon juice, and season salad

3. In another bowl, toss cabbage with vinegar

4. In each pita pocket, add hummus, eggplant and drizzle tahini sauce

5. Top with eggs, tahini sauce

Nutrition:

- Calories: 269;
- Carbohydrate: 2 g;
- Cholesterol: 3 mg;
- Fat: 14 g;
- Fiber: 2 g;
- Protein: 7 g

Salmon With Vegetables

Preparation Time: 10 minutes
Cooking Time: 15 minutes
Servings: 4
Ingredients:

- 2 tablespoons olive oil
- 2 carrots
- 1 head fennel
- 2 squash
- ¼ onion
- 1-inch ginger
- 1 cup white wine
- 2 cups water
- 2 parsley sprigs
- 2 tarragon sprigs
- 6 oz. salmon fillets
- 1 cup cherry tomatoes
- 1 scallion

Directions:

1. In a skillet, heat olive oil, add fennel, squash, onion, ginger, carrot, and cook until vegetables are soft.

2. Add wine, water, parsley and cook for another 4–5 minutes.

3. Season salmon fillets and place them in the pan.

4. Cook on one side for 5 minutes.

5. Transfer salmon to a bowl, spoon tomatoes and scallion around salmon, and serve.

Nutrition:
- Calories: 301;
- Carbohydrate: 2 g;
- Cholesterol: 13 mg;
- Fat: 17 g;
- Fiber: 4 g;
- Protein: 8 g

Crispy Fish

Preparation Time: 5 minutes
Cooking Time: 15 minutes
Servings: 4
Ingredients:

- Thick fish fillets

- ¼ cup all-purpose flour

- 1 egg

- 1 cup breadcrumbs

- 2 tablespoons vegetables

- Lemon wedge

Directions:

1. In a dish, add flour, egg, breadcrumbs in different dishes and set aside.

2. Dip each fish fillet into the flour, egg, and then breadcrumbs bowl.

3. Place each fish fillet in a heated skillet and cook for 4–5 minutes per side.

4. Remove from the pan when ready and serve with lemon wedges.

Nutrition:

- Calories: 189;
- Carbohydrate: 2 g;
- Cholesterol: 73 mg;
- Fat: 17 g;
- Fiber: 0 g;
- Protein: 7 g;

Moules Mariners

Preparation Time: 10 minutes
Cooking Time: 30 minutes
Servings: 4
Ingredients:

- 2 tablespoons unsalted butter

- 1 leek

- 1 shallot

- 2 cloves garlic

- 2 bay leaves

- 1 cup white wine

- 2 lb. mussels

- 2 tablespoons mayonnaise

- 1 tablespoon lemon zest

- 2 tablespoons parsley

- 1 sourdough bread

Directions:

1. In a saucepan, melt butter, add leeks, garlic, bay leaves, shallot, and cook until vegetables are soft.

2. Bring to a boil, add mussels, and cook for 1–2 minutes,

3. Transfer mussels to a bowl and cover.

4. Whisk in remaining butter with mayonnaise and return mussels to the pot.

5. Add lemon juice, parsley, lemon zest, and stir to combine.

Nutrition:

- Calories: 321;

- Carbohydrate: 2 g;
- Cholesterol: 13 mg;
- Fat: 17 g;
- Fiber: 2 g;
- Protein: 9 g

Steamed Mussels with Coconut-Curry

Preparation Time: 15 minutes
Cooking Time: 20 minutes
Servings: 4
Ingredients:

- 6 sprigs cilantro

- 2 garlic cloves

- 2 shallots

- ¼ teaspoon coriander seeds

- ¼ teaspoon red chili flakes

- 1 teaspoon zest

- 1 can coconut milk

- 1 tablespoon vegetable oil

- 1 tablespoon curry paste

- 1 tablespoon brown sugar

- 1 tablespoon fish sauce

- 2 lb. mussels

Directions:

1. In a bowl, combine lime zest, cilantro stems, shallot, garlic, coriander seed, chili, and salt.

2. In a saucepan, heat oil and add garlic, shallots, pounded paste, and curry paste.

3. Cook for 3–4 minutes, add coconut milk, sugar, and fish sauce.

4. Bring to a simmer and add mussels.

5. Stir in lime juice, cilantro leaves and cook for a couple of more minutes.

6. When ready, remove from heat and serve.

Nutrition:
- Calories: 209;
- Carbohydrate: 6 g;
- Cholesterol: 13 mg;
- Fat: 7 g;
- Fiber: 2 g;
- Protein: 17 g

Tuna Noodle Casserole

Preparation Time: 15 minutes
Cooking Time: 20 minutes
Servings: 4
Ingredients:

- 2 oz. egg noodles

- 4 oz. fraiche

- 1 egg

- 1 teaspoon cornstarch

- 1 tablespoon juice from 1 lemon

- 1 can tuna

- 1 cup peas

- ¼ cup parsley

Directions:

1. Place noodles in a saucepan with water and bring to a boil.

2. In a bowl, combine egg, crème Fraiche and lemon juice, and whisk well.

3. When noodles are cooked, add crème Fraiche mixture to the skillet and mix well.

4. Add tuna, peas, parsley lemon juice, and mix well.

5. When ready, remove from heat and serve.

Nutrition:

- Calories: 214;
- Carbohydrate: 2 g;
- Cholesterol: 73 mg;
- Fat: 7 g;
- Protein: 19 g

CHICKEN

Lean and Green Chicken Pesto Pasta

Preparation Time: 5 minutes
Cooking Time: 10 minutes
Servings: 1
1 Fueling, 1 Healthy Fat, 1/2 Lean, 1 Green, 1 Condiment
Ingredients:
- 3 cups raw kale leaves
- 2 tbsp. olive oil
- 2 cups fresh basil
- 1/4 teaspoon salt
- 3 tbsp. lemon juice
- 3 garlic cloves
- 2 cups cooked chicken breast
- 1 cup baby Broccoli
- 6 ounces uncooked chicken pasta
- 3 ounces diced fresh mozzarella
- Basil leaves or red pepper flakes to garnish

Directions:
1. Start by making the pesto; add the kale, lemon juice, basil, garlic cloves, olive oil, and salt to a blender and blend until it's smooth.

2. Add salt and pepper to taste.

3. Cook the pasta and strain off the water. Reserve 1/4 cup of the liquid.

4. Get a bowl and mix everything, the cooked pasta, pesto, diced chicken, Broccoli, mozzarella, and the reserved pasta liquid.

5. Sprinkle the mixture with additional chopped basil or red paper flakes (optional).

6. Now your salad is ready. You may serve it warm or chilled. Also, it can be taken as a salad mix-ins or as a side dish. Leftovers should be stored in the refrigerator inside an air-tight container for 3-5 days.

Nutrition:
- Calories: 244,
- Fats: 10g,
- Proteins: 20.5g,
- Carbohydrates: 22.5g

Yogurt Garlic Chicken

Preparation Time: 30 minutes
Cooking Time: 60 minutes
Servings: 6
Ingredients:

- 6 pieces Pita bread rounds halved

- 1 cup English cucumber, sliced thinly, w/ each slice halved

Chicken & vegetables:

- 3 tablespoons Olive oil

- 1/2 teaspoon Black pepper, freshly ground

- 20 ounces Chicken thighs, skinless, boneless

- 1 piece Bell pepper, red, sliced into half-inch portions

- 4 pieces Garlic cloves, chopped finely

- 1/2 teaspoon Cuminutes, ground

- 1 piece Red onion, medium, sliced into half-inch wedges

- 1/2 cup Yogurt, plain, fat-free

- 2 tablespoons Lemon juice

- 1 ½ teaspoon Salt

- 1/2 teaspoon Red pepper flakes, crushed

- 1/2 teaspoon Allspice, ground

- 1 piece Bell pepper, yellow, sliced into half-inch portions

Yogurt sauce:

- 2 tablespoons Olive oil

- 1/4 teaspoon salt

- 1 tablespoon Parsley, flat-leaf, chopped finely

- 1 cup Yogurt, plain, fat-free

- 1 tablespoon Lemon juice, fresh

- 1 piece Garlic clove, chopped finely

Directions:

1. Mix the yogurt (1/2 cup), garlic cloves (4 pieces), olive oil (1 tablespoon), salt (1 teaspoon), lemon juice (2 tablespoons), pepper (1/4 teaspoon), allspice, minutes, and pepper flakes. Stir in the chicken and coat well. Cover and marinate for two hours in the fridge.

2. Preheat the air fryer to 400 ° Fahrenheit.

3. Grease a rimmed baking sheet (18x13-inch) with cooking spray.

4. Toss the bell peppers and onion with remaining olive oil (2 tablespoons), pepper (1/4 teaspoon), and salt (1/2 teaspoon).

5. Arrange veggies on the baking sheets left side and the marinated chicken thighs (drain first) on the right side—Cook in the air fryer for 25 to 30 minutes.

6. Mix the yogurt sauce ingredients.

7. Slice air-fried chicken into half-inch strips.

8. Top each pita round with chicken strips, roasted veggies, cucumbers, and yogurt sauce.

Nutrition:

- Calories: 380,
- Fat: 10g,
- Proteins: 20g,
- Carbohydrates: 30g

Bacon Wings

Preparation Time: 15 minutes
Cooking Time: 1 hour 15 minutes
Servings: 12
Ingredients:

- 12 pieces bacon strips

- 1 teaspoon Paprika

- 1 tablespoon Black pepper

- 1 teaspoon Oregano

- 12 pieces Chicken wings

- 1 tablespoon Kosher salt

- 1 tablespoon Brown sugar

- 1 teaspoon Chili powder

- Celery sticks

- Blue cheese dressing

Directions:

1. Preheat the air fryer to 325 ° Fahrenheit.

2. Mix sugar, salt, chili powder, oregano, pepper, and paprika. Coat chicken wings with this dry rub.

3. Wrap a bacon strip around each wing. Arrange wrapped wings in the air fryer basket.

4. Cook for 30 minutes on each side in the air fryer. Let cool for 5 minutes.

5. Serve and enjoy with celery and blue cheese.

Nutrition:

- Calories: 200,
- Fats: 12g,
- Proteins: 15g,
- Carbohydrates: 6g

Buffalo Chicken Sliders

Preparation Time: 10 minutes
Cooking Time: 15 minutes
Servings: 12
Ingredients:

- 2lb Chicken breasts, cooked, shredded

- 1 cup Wing sauce

- 1 pack Ranch dressing mix

- 1/4 cup, low-fat Blue cheese dressing

- Lettuce (for topping)

- 12, slider buns

Directions:

1. Add the chicken breasts (shredded, cooked) in a large bowl along with the ranch dressing and wing sauce.

2. Stir well to combine, then place a piece of lettuce onto each slider roll.

3. Top off using the chicken mixture.

4. Drizzle blue cheese dressing over chicken, then top off using top buns of slider rolls.

5. Serve.

Nutrition:

- Calories: 300,
- Fats: 14 g,
- Cholesterol: 25 mg

High Proteins Chicken Meatballs

Preparation Time: 5 minutes
Cooking Time: 25 minutes
Servings: 2
Ingredients:

- 1 lbs. Chicken (lean, ground)
- 3/4 cup Oats (rolled)
- Onions (2, grated)
- 2 tsp. Allspice (ground)
- Salt and black pepper (dash)

Directions:

1. Heat a skillet (large) over medium heat, then grease using cooking spray.

2. Add in the onions (grated), chicken (lean, ground), oats (rolled), allspice (earth), and a dash of salt and black pepper in a large-sized bowl. Stir well to combine.

3. Shape mixture into meatballs (small).

4. Place into the skillet (greased). Cook for about 5 minutes until all sides are golden brown.

5. Remove meatballs from heat, then serve immediately.

Nutrition:

- Calories: 519,
- Fats: 15g,
- Proteins: 57g,
- Carbohydrates: 32g

Garlicky Tomato Chicken Casserole

Preparation Time: 5 minutes
Cooking Time: 50 minutes
Servings: 4
Ingredients:

- 4 chicken breasts

- 2 tomatoes, sliced.

- 1 can diced tomatoes.

- 2 garlic cloves, chopped.

- 1 shallot, chopped.

- 1 bay leaf

- 1 thyme sprig

- ½ cup dry white wine

- ½ cup chicken stock

- Salt and pepper to taste.

Directions:

1. Combine the chicken and the remaining ingredients in a deep dish baking pan.

2. Adjust the taste with salt and pepper and cover the pot with a lid or aluminum foil.

3. Cook in the preheated oven at 330°F for 40 minutes.

4. Serve the casserole warm.

Nutrition:

- Calories: 313,
- Fats: 8g,
- Proteins: 47g,
- Carbohydrates: 6g

Chicken Omelet

Preparation Time: 5 minutes
Cooking Time: 15 minutes
Servings: 1
Ingredients:

- 2 bacon slices; cooked and crumbled.

- 2 eggs

- 1 tablespoon homemade mayonnaise

- 1 tomato; chopped.

- 1-ounce rotisserie chicken; shredded

- 1 teaspoon mustard

- 1 small Almond; pitted, peeled, and chopped.

- Salt and black pepper to the taste

Directions:

1. In a bowl, mix eggs with some salt and pepper and whisk gently.

2. Heat up a pan over medium heat; spray with some cooking oil, add eggs and cook your omelet for 5 minutes.

3. Add chicken, Almond, tomato, bacon, mayo, and mustard on one half of the omelet.

4. Fold omelet, cover the pan and cook for 5 minutes more. Transfer to a plate and serve!

Nutrition:

- Calories: 400,
- Fats: 3g,
- Fibers: 6g,
- Carbohydrates: 4g,
- Proteins: 25g

Chicken Cacciatore

Preparation Time: 5 minutes
Cooking Time: 45 minutes
Servings: 6
Ingredients:

- 2 tablespoons extra virgin olive oil

- 6 chicken thighs

- 1 sweet onion, chopped.

- 2 garlic cloves, minced

- 2 red bell peppers, cored and diced

- 2 carrots, diced

- 1 rosemary sprig

- 1 thyme sprig

- 4 tomatoes, peeled and diced

- ½ cup tomato juice

- ¼ cup dry white wine

- 1 cup chicken stock

- 1 bay leaf

- Salt and pepper to taste

Directions:

1. Heat the oil in a heavy saucepan.

2. Cook chicken on all sides until golden.

3. Stir in the garlic and onion and cook for 2 minutes.

4. Stir in the rest of the ingredients and season with salt and pepper.

5. Cook on low heat for 30 minutes.

6. Serve the chicken cacciatore warm and fresh.

Nutrition:
- Calories: 363,
- Fats: 14g,
- Proteins: 42g,
- Carbohydrates: 9g

SOUP

Cheeseburger Soup

Preparation Time: 10 minutes
Cooking Time: 40 minutes
Servings: 4 Servings
1 Lean, 3 Green, 1 Fat, 3 Condiments
Ingredients:

- 3 cups of water

- 1 pound lean ground beach

- 1 cup celery, diced

- 1 teaspoon parsley

- 1/2 onion, chopped

- 2 cups peeled and diced potatoes, optional

- 1 teaspoon dried basil

- 1 (14.5-oz) can diced tomatoes

- Salt and pepper to taste

- 1 1/2 teaspoons plain, low-fat Greek yogurt

- 1 bunch spinach, torn

- 1 cup low-fat goat cheese, grated

Directions:

1. Brown the beef in a large soup pot.

2. Add the chopped onion, parsley, basil, and celery and sauté for a couple of minutes until tender. Remove beef from the heat and then drain off any excess fat.

3. Add in the water, tomatoes, potatoes (if using), yogurt, salt, and pepper. Cover and simmer for 20 minutes on low until potatoes are fork-tender.

4. Add in the spinach and cook for 2 minutes until wilted.

5. Serve topped with cheese. Have fun!

Nutrition:
- Calories: 401g;
- Protein: 44.2g;
- Fat: 20.3g;
- Carbs: 11g

Creamy Cauliflower Soup

Preparation Time: 15 minutes
Cooking Time: 15 minutes
Servings: 6
Ingredients:

- 5 cups of cauliflower rice

- 8 oz. of Cheddar cheese; grated

- 2 cups of unsweetened almond milk

- 2 cups of vegetable stock

- 2 tbsps. of water

- 1 small onion; chopped

- 2 garlic cloves; minced

- 1 tbsp. of olive oil

- Pepper

- Salt

Directions:

1. Heat olive oil over medium heat in a large stockpot.

2. Add onion and garlic and cook for 1–2 minutes.

3. Add cauliflower rice and water. Cover and cook for 5–7 minutes.

4. Now add vegetable stock and almond milk and stir well. Bring to a boil.

5. Turn heat to low and simmer for 5 minutes.

6. Turn off the heat. Slowly add Cheddar and stir until smooth.

7. Season soup with pepper and salt.

8. Stir well and serve hot.

Nutrition:
- Calories: 214;
- Fat: 15 g;
- Carbs: 3 g;
- Sugar: 3 g;
- Protein: 16 g;
- Cholesterol: 40 mg

Asparagus Avocado Soup

Preparation Time: 10 minutes
Cooking Time: 20 minutes
Servings: 4
Ingredients:

- 1 avocado; peeled, pitted, cubed

- 12 ounces of asparagus

- ½ teaspoon of ground black pepper

- 1 teaspoon of garlic powder

- 1 teaspoon of sea salt

- 2 tablespoons of olive oil; divided

- 1/2 of a lemon; juiced

- 2 cups of vegetable stock

Directions:

1. Switch on the air fryer, insert fryer basket, grease it with olive oil, shut with its lid, set the fryer at 425°F, and preheat for 5 minutes.

2. Meanwhile, place asparagus in a shallow dish, drizzle with 1 tablespoon of oil, sprinkle with garlic powder, salt, black pepper, and toss until it is well mixed.

3. Open the fryer, put asparagus inside it, close with its lid, and cook for 10 minutes or until nicely golden and roasted, shaking halfway through the frying.

4. When the air-fryer beeps, open its lid and transfer asparagus to a food processor.

5. Add the remaining ingredients into a food processor and pulse until well minced and smooth.

6. Tip the soup in a saucepan, pour in water if the soup is just too thick, and heat it over medium-low heat for 5 minutes or until thoroughly heated.

7. Ladle soup into bowls and serve.

Nutrition:
- Calories: 208;
- Carbs: 2 g;
- Fat: 11 g;
- Protein: 4 g;
- Fiber: 5 g

Homemade Chicken Broth

Preparation Time: 5 minutes
Cooking Time: 30 minutes
Servings: 4
Ingredients:

- 1 tablespoon of olive oil

- 1 chopped onion

- 2 chopped stalks celery

- 2 chopped carrots

- 1 whole chicken

- 2 ¼ water

- 1 tablespoon salt

- ½ teaspoon pepper

- 1 teaspoon fresh sage

Directions:

1. Sauté vegetables in oil.

2. Mix chicken and water and simmer for 2+ hours or until the chicken falls off the bone. Keep adding water as required.

3. Remove the chicken meat from the broth, place it on a platter, and let it cool. Pull chicken off the carcass and put it into the broth.

4. Pour broth mixture into pint and quart mason jars. Make sure to add meat to every jar.

5. Leave one full inch of space from the top of the jar, or it will crack when it freezes and liquids expand. Jars can stay in the freezer for up to a year.

6. Take out and use whenever you make a soup.

Nutrition:
- Calories: 213;
- Fat: 6 g;
- Fiber: 13 g;
- Carbs: 16 g;
- Protein: 22 g

Fish Stew

Preparation Time: 5 minutes
Cooking Time: 30 minutes
Servings: 4
Ingredients:

- 1 tablespoon of olive oil

- 1 chopped onion or leek

- 2 chopped stalks celery

- 2 chopped carrots

- 1 clove of minced garlic

- 1 tablespoon of parsley

- 1 bay leaf

- 1 clove

- 1/8 teaspoon of kelp or dulse (seaweed)

- ¼ teaspoon of salt

- Fish—leftover, cooked, diced

- 2–3 cups of chicken or vegetable broth

Directions:

1. Mix all of the ingredients and simmer on the stove for 20 minutes.

Nutrition:

- Calories: 342;
- Fat: 15 g;
- Fiber: 11 g;
- Carbs: 8 g;
- Protein: 10 g

Roasted Tomato and Seafood Stew

Preparation Time: 10 minutes
Cooking Time: 46 minutes
Servings: 6
Ingredients:

- 2 tablespoons of extra-virgin olive oil
- 1 yellow onion; diced
- 1 fennel bulb; tops removed, and bulb diced
- 3 garlic cloves; minced
- 1 cup of dry white wine
- 2 (14.5-ounce) cans of fire-roasted tomatoes
- 2 cups of chicken stock
- 1-pound of medium (21-30 count) shrimp; peeled and deveined
- 1-pound of raw white fish (cod or haddock); cubed
- Salt
- Freshly ground black pepper
- Fresh basil; torn, for garnish

Directions:

1. Select Roast/to sauté and set to Med. Press Start/stop to start. Allow preheating for 3 minutes.
2. Add the olive oil, onions, fennel, and garlic. Cook until translucent or around 3 minutes.

3. Add the wine and deglaze, scraping any stuck bits from the pot's bottom using a silicone spatula. Add the roasted tomatoes and chicken broth. Simmer for 25 to 30 minutes. Add the shrimp and whitefish.

4. Select Roast/to sauté and set to Medium-low. Press Start/stop to start.

5. Simmer for 10 minutes, stirring regularly, until the fish and shrimp are thoroughly cooked.

64

6. Season with salt and pepper.

7. Ladle into a bowl and serve topped with torn basil.

Nutrition:
- Calories: 301;
- Total fat: 8 g;
- Saturated Fat: 1 g;
- Cholesterol: 99 mg;
- Sodium: 808 mg;
- Carbohydrates: 21 g;
- Fiber: 4 g;
- Protein: 26 g

SALAD

Lemon Greek Salad

Preparation Time: 25 minutes
Cooking Time: 25 minutes
Servings: 1
Ingredients:

- 140 oz Chicken breast

- 1 cup Chopped cucumber

- 1 cup Chopped orange/red bell pepper

- 1 cup Wedged/sliced/chopped tomatoes

- 1/4 cup Chopped olives

- 2 tablespoons fresh parsley (finely chopped)

- 2 tablespoons Finely chopped red onion

- 5 teaspoons Lemon juice

- 1 teaspoon Olive oil

- 1 minced garlic clove

Direction:

1. Preheat your grill to medium heat.
2. Grill the chicken and cook on each side until it is no longer pink or for 5 minutes.
3. Cut the chicken into tiny pieces. In your serving bowl, mix garlic, olives, and parsley. Whisk in olive oil (1 teaspoon) and lemon juice (4 teaspoons). Add onion, tomatoes, bell pepper, and cucumber.
4. Toss gently. Coat the ingredients with dressing. Add another teaspoon of lemon juice to taste. Divide the salad into two servings and put 6oz chicken on top of each salad.
5. Enjoy your meal.

Nutrition:

- Protein: 56g;
- Fiber: 4g;
- Carbs: 14g;
- Sodium: 280mg;
- Fat: 12g;
- Calories: 380

Broccoli Salad

Preparation Time: 5 minutes
Cooking Time: 25 minutes
Servings: 1
Ingredients:

- 1/3 tablespoons sherry vinegar

- 1/24 cup olive oil

- 1/3 teaspoons fresh thyme, chopped

- 1/6 teaspoon Dijon mustard

- 1/6 teaspoon honey

- Salt to taste

- 1 1/3 cups broccoli florets

- 1/3 red onions

- 1/12 cup parmesan cheese, shaved

- 1/24 cup pecans

Directions:

1. Mix the sherry vinegar, olive oil, thyme, mustard, honey, and salt in a bowl.
2. In a serving bowl, blend the broccoli florets and onions.
3. Drizzle the dressing on top.
4. Sprinkle with the pecans and parmesan cheese before serving.

Nutrition:

- Calories: 199;
- Fat: 17.4g;
- Carbohydrates: 7.5g;
- Fiber: 2.8g;
- Protein: 5.2g

Potato Carrot Salad

Preparation Time: 15 minutes
Cooking Time: 10 minutes
Servings: 1
Ingredients:

- Water

- 1 potato, sliced into cubes

- 1/2 carrots, cut into cubes

- 1/6 tablespoon milk

- 1/6 tablespoon Dijon mustard

- 1/24 cup mayonnaise

- Pepper to taste

- 1/3 teaspoons fresh thyme, chopped

- 1/6 stalk celery, chopped

- 1/6 scallions, chopped

- 1/6 slice turkey bacon, cooked crispy and crumbled

Directions:

1. Fill your pot with water.
2. Place it over medium-high heat.
3. Boil the potatoes and carrots for 10 to 12 minutes or until tender.
4. Drain and let cool.
5. In a bowl, mix the milk, mustard, mayonnaise, pepper, and thyme.
6. Stir in the potatoes, carrots, and celery.
7. Coat evenly with the sauce.
8. Cover and refrigerate for 4 hours.
9. Top with the scallions and turkey bacon bits before serving.

Nutrition:

- Calories: 106;
- Fat: 5.3g;
- Carbohydrates: 12.6g;
- Fiber: 1.8g;
- Protein: 2g

Marinated Veggie Salad

Preparation Time: 4 hours and 30 minutes
Cooking Time: 3 minutes
Servings: 1
Ingredients:

- 1 zucchini, sliced

- 4 tomatoes, sliced into wedges

- ¼ cup red onion, sliced thinly

- 1 green bell pepper, sliced

- 2 tablespoons fresh parsley, chopped

- 2 tablespoons red-wine vinegar

- 2 tablespoons olive oil

- 1 garlic clove, minced

- 1 teaspoon dried basil

- 2 tablespoons water

- Pine nuts, toasted and chopped

Directions:

1. In a bowl, combine the zucchini, tomatoes, red onion, green bell pepper, and parsley.
2. Pour the vinegar and oil into a glass jar with a lid.
3. Add the garlic, basil, and water.
4. Seal the jar and stir well to combine.
5. Pour the dressing into the vegetable mixture.
6. Cover the bowl.
7. Marinate in the refrigerator for 4 hours.
8. Garnish with the pine nuts before serving.

Nutrition:

- Calories: 65;

- Fat: 4.7g;
- Saturated fat: 0.7g;
- Carbohydrates: 5.3g;
- Fiber: 1.2g;
- Protein: 0.9g

Mediterranean Salad

Preparation Time: 20 minutes
Cooking Time: 5 minutes
Servings: 1
Ingredients:

- 1 teaspoon balsamic vinegar

- 1/2 tablespoon basil pesto

- 1/2 cup lettuce

- 1/8 cup broccoli florets, chopped

- 1/8 cup zucchini, chopped

- 1/8 cup tomato, chopped

- 1/8 cup yellow bell pepper, chopped

- 1/2 tablespoons feta cheese, crumbled

Directions:

1. Arrange the lettuce on a serving platter.
2. Top with broccoli, zucchini, tomato, and bell pepper.
3. In a bowl, mix the vinegar and pesto.
4. Drizzle the dressing on top.
5. Sprinkle the feta cheese and serve.

Nutrition:

- Calories: 100;
- Fat: 6g;
- Saturated fat: 1g;
- Carbohydrates: 7g;
- Protein: 4g

SIDE DISHES

Turmeric Roasted Cauliflower Bites

Preparation Time: 10 minutes
Cooking Time: 35 minutes
Servings: 4
1 Healthy fat, 3 Greens, 3 Condiments
Ingredients:

- 1 1/2 heads cauliflower, cut into florets

- 4 teaspoons canola oil

- 1/2 teaspoon turmeric

- 1/2 teaspoon cayenne

- 1 lemon, juiced

- 1 1/2 teaspoons curry powder

- 2 garlic cloves, minced

- 1/2 teaspoon each of salt and ground black pepper

Directions:

1. Preheat the oven to 450 °F.

2. Using a big zip-lock bag to put all the ingredients. Toss until well combined.

3. Arrange the cauliflower on a single layer on a foil-lined baking sheet. Roast for about 30–35 minutes, occasionally stirring until tender and golden brown. Serve and enjoy!

Nutrition:

- Calories: 78;
- Net carbs: 3g;
- Fiber: 2g;
- Protein: 2.5g;
- Fat: 4.9g

Mashed Cauliflower with Mushroom Gravy

Preparation Time: 5 minutes
Cooking Time: 20 minutes
Servings: 4
2 Green, 1 Healthy Fat, 3 Condiments
Ingredients:
For the Mashed Cauliflower:
- 4 cups cauliflower florets
- 1 tablespoon extra-virgin olive oil
- 1 teaspoon garlic powder
- 3/4 cup light cream cheese, softened
- 1 tablespoon sage, minced
- 1 tablespoon fresh rosemary, minced
- Salt and pepper to taste
- 1 teaspoon dried paprika

For the Gravy:
- 1 tablespoon canola oil
- 1/4 tablespoon tamari
- 1/3 cup finely chopped shallot
- 8 ounces cremini mushrooms, sliced
- 1 garlic clove, minced
- 3/4 tablespoon fresh thyme leaves
- 1/4 teaspoon chopped rosemary
- 1/8 cup all-purpose flour
- 1 1/2 cups chicken broth

- Sea salt and black pepper to taste

Directions:
1. To a boil, put a big saucepan of water.

2. To fork-tender, boil the cauliflower florets for 10 minutes. Drain and set aside slightly to cool.

3. Add the cooled cauliflower and the remaining cauliflower ingredients in a food processor and process until smooth. Set aside.

4. Heat the oil in a skillet over medium heat to render the gravy. Add the shallot and cook until tender, for about 4 minutes.

5. Add the mushrooms and cook for 8 minutes until soft. Stir in the garlic, tamari, thyme, and rosemary. Sprinkle the flour over the mushrooms and stir for a minute.

6. Add the broth and simmer until thickened, continually stirring, for 20 minutes.

7. Season with salt and pepper to taste.

8. Serve gravy over mashed cauliflower.

9. Have fun!

Nutrition:
- Calories: 324;
- Fat: 25g;
- Protein: 21g;
- Carbs: 27g

Chips and Chicken Cheese Dip

Preparation Time: 15 minutes
Cooking Time: 45 minutes
Servings: 4
1 Leaner, 3 Green, 1 Healthy Fat, 3 Condiments
Ingredients:
For the Chips

- 4 large zucchini, sliced 1/4 inch thick

- 1 teaspoon lemon juice

- 1/2 teaspoon smoked paprika

- 1 tablespoon canola oil

- 1/2 teaspoon minutes

- 1/2 teaspoon pepper

- 1/2 teaspoon sea salt

For the Dip:

- 1 1/2 cup plain, reduced-fat Greek yogurt

- 4 light cheese wedges, softened

- 1 (12.5 oz) can chicken breast, drained

- 1/4 cup hot sauce

- 1/3 cup ranch dressing

- 1 cup shredded low-fat Cheddar cheese

Directions:
1. Lay the slices of zucchini in a single layer on paper towels. Cover and set a heavy item on top of the slices with more paper towels. Press down on the object to help squeeze out some of the moisture.

2. Preheat the oven to 400°F.

3. Combine the oil, lemon, paprika, minutes, salt, and pepper in a bowl.

4. Add the zucchini slices, and gently mix to coat.

5. Lightly grease a large baking sheet and then arrange the zucchini sliced on the sheet in a single layer.

6. Bake for about 30 minutes or until crisp and golden.

7. While chips are baking, combine all the ingredients for the dip in a blender, and blend until smooth.

8. Move the mixture to a lightly greased baking dish and cook for 15 minutes in the oven or until lightly browned.

9. Serve and enjoy!

Nutrition:
- Calories: 341;
- Carbs: 15g;
- Protein: 35g;
- Fat: 14g

Asparagus Risotto

Preparation Time: 10 minutes
Cooking Time: 20 minutes
Servings: 4
1 Leaner, 1 Healthy Fat, 3 Green, 2 Condiments
Ingredients:

- 1 cup asparagus, trimmed, chopped into small lengths

- 3 tablespoons nutritional yeast

- 2 pounds turkey breasts, boneless and skinless

- 1/4 teaspoon sea salt

- 2 tablespoons + 1/2 teaspoon extra virgin olive oil

- 1/4 teaspoon ground black pepper

- 5 cups grated cauliflower

- 1/2 cup beef broth

- 1 teaspoon dried thyme, chopped

- 1 teaspoon dried paprika

- 4 oz mushrooms, sliced (optional)

- 1 tablespoon chopped cilantro

Directions:

1. Preheat your oven to 350°F.

2. Combine the 2 tablespoons of oil, thyme, paprika, salt, and pepper in a small bowl. Rub the mixture all over the turkey. Place the turkey in a cooking dish and then sprinkle with 1/2 teaspoon olive oil.

3. Roast the turkey in the oven for about 35 minutes or until a thermometer inserted reads 165 F. Remove from the oven and allow to rest.

4. Meanwhile, add the asparagus, grated cauliflower, mushroom (if using), and broth in a pot and simmer on a stovetop until tender, adding more broth as needed.

5. Remove the asparagus risotto from the heat and stir in the yeast and cilantro.

6. You can serve asparagus risotto as a side or with roasted turkey (if desired) as the main dish.

Nutrition:
- Calories: 432;
- Protein: 56g;
- Carbs: 11.1g;
- Fat: 17.3g

Kale Mashed Potatoes

Preparation Time: 5 minutes
Cooking Time: 10 minutes
Servings: 2
1 Fueling, 1 Healthy Fat, 1/2 Lean, 1 Green, 1 Condiment
Ingredients:

- 1 cup low-fat Cheddar cheese, shredded

- 2 cups fresh kale

- 1 tablespoon low-fat cream cheese

- 2 packets Optavia Essential Roasted Garlic Creamy Smashed Potatoes

Directions:

1. Prepare the Smashed Potatoes following package instructions. Set aside.

2. Trim the kale, discarding the thick ribs and stems, and then chop leaves.

3. Get it to a boil with a pot of water. Place chopped kale in a steamer basket and place the basket over the simmering water. Cover with a lid and let it steam for about 5 minutes or until tender.

4. In a bowl, combine the roasted smashed potatoes, steamed kale, and shredded cheese.

5. Serve topped with cream cheese

Nutrition:

- Calories: 324;
- Protein: 25g;
- Fat: 15.7g;
- Carbs: 30g.

KULTURE
KITCHEN

PUBLISHING HOUSE

THE COMPLETE
LEAN

GREEN
DIET COOKBOOK

Cookbook 2

The Power of Fueling Hacks Meals Vol. 2

Audrey Chambers

MEAT

Orange Beef Broccoli

Preparation Time: 10 minutes
Cooking Time: 10 minutes
Servings: 4
Ingredients:

- 4 tsp Orange oil (or any other oil and grated orange peel)

- 1 1/2 lbs. London broil (lean, thinly sliced)

- 4 cup Broccoli florets

- 1 tablespoon Thai seasoning

- 1/4 cup Beef stock

- Seasoning (salt & pepper) - pinch

Directions:

1. Add the orange oil to a pan and heat over high heat. Add the beef to the pan and cook for around 3 minutes on each side.

2. Add the Thai seasoning, broccoli, and beef stock, and cover the pan.

3. Reduce heat and simmer for about 5 minutes or until the broccoli becomes crispy and tender.

4. Open the pan and simmer for extra 2 minutes to reduce the liquid by half.

Nutrition:

- Calories: 360kcal;
- Fat: 14g;
- Carbohydrates: 6g;
- Sugar: 1.6g;
- Protein: 49.4g

Ground Beef Joes

Preparation Time: 5 minutes
Cooking Time: 25 minutes
Servings: 4
Ingredients:

- 1 1/2 pounds Lean ground beef

- 1/2 cup Green bell pepper (diced)

- 2 tablespoons Tomato paste

- 1 teaspoon Powdered stevia

- 1 tablespoon yellow mustard

- 1 tablespoon Garlic Gusto seasoning

- 1/2 tablespoon Cinnamon chipotle seasoning

- 1 tablespoon Red wine vinegar

- 1 cup Beef broth (low sodium)

- Salt and pepper to taste

Directions:

1. Add the beef to your pan and cook over medium heat for about 7 minutes.

2. While cooking, break the beef into smaller pieces.

3. Except for the broth, add other ingredients and stir thoroughly to combine well.

4. Then add the broth and increase the heat to medium-high heat.

5. Lower the heat to low once it started boiling and simmer for about 15 minutes with the pot uncovered.

6. Serve.

Nutrition:
- Calories: 302kcal;
- Fat: 11.5g;
- Carbohydrates: 2.7g;
- Fiber: 0.6g;
- Sugar: 1g;
- Protein: 44.1g

Cauliflower-Turkey Burger

Preparation Time: 10 minutes
Cooking Time: 20 minutes
Serves: 1
Ingredients:

- 5 ounces ground turkey

- 1 cup Cauliflower florets

- 1 1/4 cups Chicken broth

- 1/2 teaspoon Garlic clove (minced)

- 1 teaspoon Cornstarch

- 1/2 cup Fresh asparagus

Directions:

1. Bring the chicken broth to a boil.

2. Add the cauliflower and cook till it becomes tender.

3. Drain and mash the cauliflower florets.

4. Add the turkey burger to your skillet and spray it with cooking spray.

5. Let the internal temperature reach 165°F.

6. Chop the turkey into smaller pieces and season with salt and pepper.

7. Meanwhile, add the remaining ¼ cup of chicken broth to a saucepan and simmer.

8. Mix the cornstarch with water and stir until it dissolves completely.

9. Remove the chicken broth from heat and add the cornstarch.

10. Whisk the mixture to thicken.

11. Add the garlic and stir well.

12. Add the asparagus to a microwave-safe plate and cover. Microwave for 45 seconds.

13. Scoop the mashed cauliflower onto the serving plate.

14. Add the turkey burger on top and spread the chicken garlic sauce over it.

15. Serve with the asparagus.

Nutrition:
- Calories: 205kcal;
- Fat: 13.2g;
- Carbohydrates: 19.1g;
- Fiber: 1.1g;
- Sugar: 7.0g;
- Protein: 28.9g

Zucchini-Pappardelle

Preparation Time: 10 minutes
Cooking Time: 30 minutes
Serves: 4
Ingredients:

- 1 1/2 lbs.Lean beef sausage (Italian seasoned)

- 2 cup Chopped tomatoes

- 1 tablespoon Garlic and spring onion seasoning

- 4 cups Zucchini noodles

- 4 teaspoons Roasted garlic oil

- 1 teaspoon Seasoning of choice

Directions:

1. Place the sausage in your pan over medium-high heat. Sauté the sausage for about 10–15 minutes. When cooking, break it up with a spatula.
2. Meanwhile, prepare the noodles and transfer them to a bowl.
3. Add the garlic seasoning and tomatoes to the sausage and stir to combine well.
4. Add the beef to the pan, cook on each side for 3 minutes. Drizzle the oil in the noodles and sprinkle over with the seasoning. Toss to coat.
5. Pour in the sausage mixture and toss thoroughly to combine well. Sprinkle grated parmesan and allowed it to sit for about 3 minutes before serving.

Nutrition:

- Calories: 308kcal;
- Fat: 12g;
- Carbohydrates: 3.7g;
- Protein: 45.1g

Tuscan Steak

Preparation Time: 10 minutes
Cooking Time: 15 minutes
Servings: 6
Ingredients:

- 1 1/2 lbs. Sirloin

- 1 tablespoon Tuscan seasoning

- 1 tablespoon Roasted garlic oil

Directions:

1. Preheat your grill to 350° F

2. Drizzle the oil over the sirloin and season both sides.

3. Place it on the grill and cook each side for about 5 minutes.

4. Let it cool down a little and remove it from the grill.

5. After about 5 minutes, slice and serve.

Nutrition:

- Calories: 130 kcal;
- Protein: 22.94 g;
- Fat: 3.32 g;
- Carbohydrates: 0.42 g

FISH AND SEAFOOD

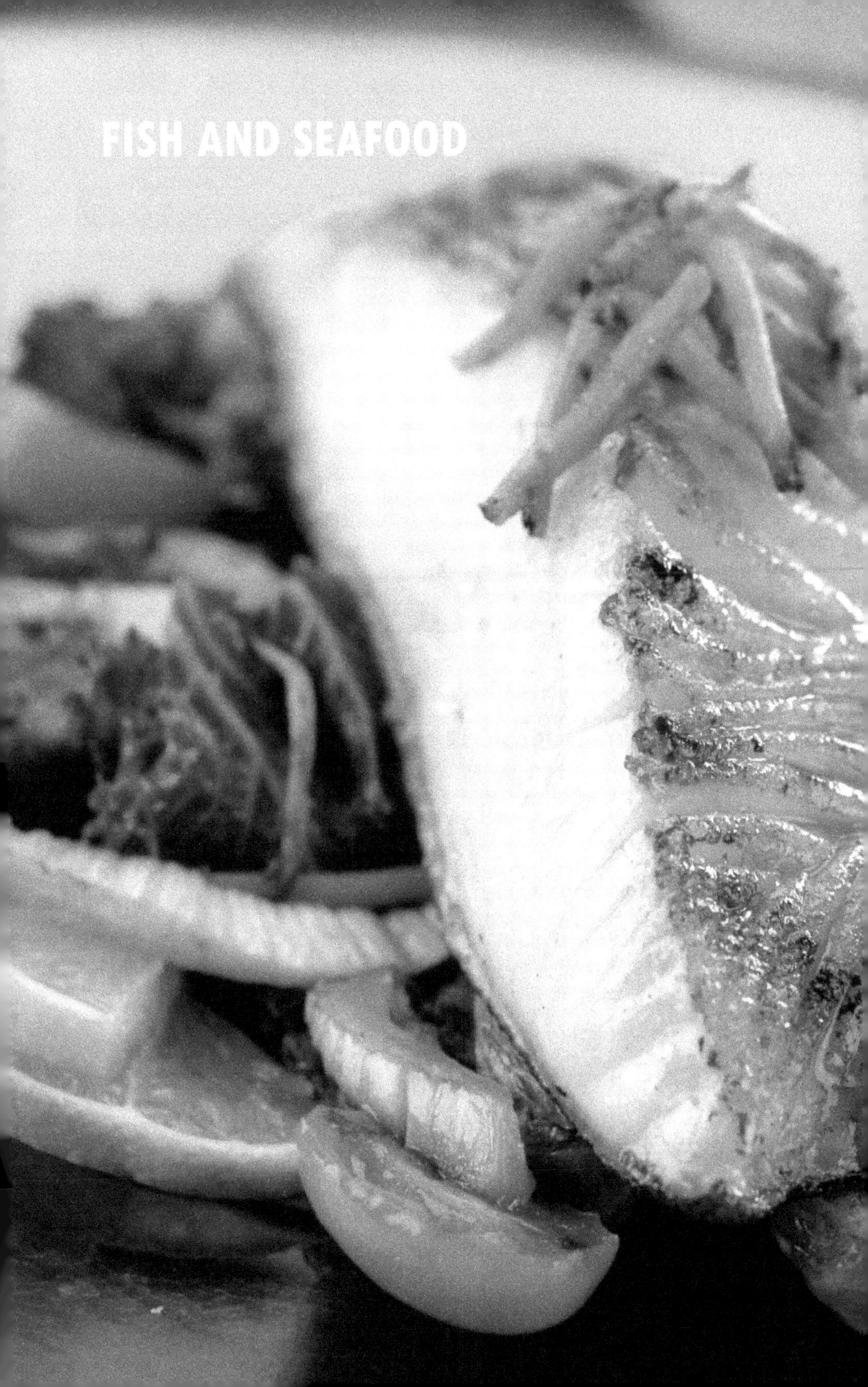

Black COD

Preparation Time: 15 minutes
Cooking Time: 20 minutes
Servings: 4
Ingredients:

- ¼ cup miso paste

- ¼ cup sake

- 1 tablespoon mirin

- 1 teaspoon soy sauce

- 1 tablespoon olive oil

- 4 black cod fillets

Directions:

1. In a bowl, combine miso, soy sauce, oil, and sake.

2. Rub mixture over cod fillets and let it marinate for 20–30 minutes.

3. Adjust broiler and broil cod filets for 10–12 minutes.

4. When fish is cooked, remove and serve.

Nutrition:

- Calories: 231;
- Carbohydrate: 2 g;
- Cholesterol: 13 mg;
- Fat: 15 g;
- Fiber: 2 g;
- Protein: 8g

Miso-Glazed Salmon

Preparation Time: 10 minutes
Cooking Time: 40 minutes
Servings: 4
Ingredients:

- ¼ cup red miso

- ¼ cup sake

- 1 tablespoon soy sauce

- 1 tablespoon vegetable oil

- 4 salmon fillets

Directions:

1. In a bowl, combine sake, oil, soy sauce, and miso.

2. Rub mixture over salmon fillets and marinate for 20–30 minutes.

3. Preheat a broiler.

4. Broil salmon for 5–10 minutes.

5. When ready, remove and serve.

Nutrition:

- Calories: 198;
- Carbohydrate: 5 g;
- Cholesterol: 12 mg;
- Total Fat: 10 g;
- Fiber: 2 g;
- Protein: 6 g;
- Sodium: 257 mg

Shrimp Curry

Preparation Time: 15 minutes
Cooking Time: 20 minutes
Servings: 4
Ingredients:

- 2 tablespoons peanut oil

- ¼ onion

- 2 garlic cloves

- 1 teaspoon ginger

- 1 teaspoon minutes

- 1 teaspoon turmeric

- 1 teaspoon paprika

- ¼ red chili powder

- 1 can tomatoes

- 1 can coconut milk

- 1 lb. peeled shrimp

- 1 tablespoon cilantro

Directions:

1. In a skillet, add onion and cook for 4–5 minutes.

2. Add ginger, minutes, garlic, chili, paprika, and cook on low heat.

3. Pour the tomatoes, coconut milk, and simmer for 10–12 minutes.

4. Stir in shrimp, cilantro, and cook for 2–3 minutes.

5. When ready, remove and serve.

Nutrition:
- Calories: 178;
- Carbohydrate: 3g;
- Cholesterol: 3 mg;
- Fat: 17 g;
- Fiber: 0g;
- Protein: 9 g

Salmon Pasta

Preparation Time: 10 minutes
Cooking Time: 25 minutes
Servings: 2
Ingredients:

- 5 tablespoons butter

- ¼ onion

- 1 tablespoon all-purpose flour

- 1 teaspoon garlic powder

- 2 cups skim milk

- ¼ cup Romano cheese

- 1 cup green peas

- ¼ cup canned mushrooms

- 8 oz. salmon

- 1 package penne pasta

Directions:

1. Carry a kettle to a boil with water.

2. Add pasta and cook for 10–12 minutes.

3. In a skillet, melt butter, add onion and sauté until tender.

4. Stir in garlic powder, flour, milk, and cheese.

5. Add mushrooms, peas and cook on low heat for 4–5 minutes.

6. Toss in salmon and cook for another 2–3 minutes.

7. When ready, serve with cooked pasta.

Nutrition:

- Calories: 211;
- Carbohydrate: 7 g;
- Cholesterol: 13 mg;
- Fat: 18 g;
- Fiber: 3 g;
- Protein: 17 g

Crab Legs

Preparation Time: 5 minutes
Cooking Time: 20 minutes
Servings: 3
Ingredients:
- 3 lb. crab legs
- ¼ cup salted butter, melted and divided
- ½ lemon, juiced
- ¼ tsp. garlic powder

Directions:
1. In a bowl, toss the crab legs and two tablespoons of the melted butter together. Place the crab legs in the basket of the fryer.
2. Cook at 400°F for 15 minutes, giving the basket a fair shake halfway through.
3. Combine the remaining butter with lemon juice and garlic powder.
4. Crack open the cooked crab legs and remove the meat. Serve with the butter dip on the side, and enjoy!

Nutrition:
- Calories: 392;
- Fat: 10g;
- Protein: 18g;
- Sugar: 8g

Crusty Pesto Salmon

Preparation Time: 5 minutes
Cooking Time: 15 minutes
Servings: 2
Ingredients:

- ¼ cup s, roughly chopped
- ¼ cup pesto
- 2 x 4-oz. salmon fillets
- 2 tbsp. unsalted butter, melted

Directions:

1. Mix the s and pesto together.
2. Place the salmon fillets in a round baking dish, roughly 6 inches in diameter.
3. Brush the fillets with butter, followed by the pesto mixture, ensuring to coat both the top and bottom. Put the baking dish inside the fryer.
4. Cook for 12 minutes at 390°F.
5. When it flakes easily when prodded with a fork, the salmon is ready. Serve it sweet.

Nutrition:

- Calories: 290;
- Fat: 11g;
- Protein: 20g;
- Sugar: 9g

Buttery Cod

Preparation Time: 10 minutes
Cooking Time: 12 minutes
Servings: 2
Ingredients:

- 2 x 4-oz. cod fillets
- 2 tbsp. salted butter, melted
- 1 tsp. Old Bay seasoning
- ½ medium lemon, sliced

Directions:

1. Place the cod fillets in a skillet.
2. Brush with melted butter, season with Old Bay, and top with a few lemon wedges.
3. Wrap the fish in aluminum foil and place it in your deep fryer.
4. Cook for 8 minutes at 350° F.
5. The cod is done when it is easily peeled. Serve hot.

Nutrition:

- Calories: 394;
- Fat: 5g;
- Protein: 12g;
- Sugar: 4g

CHICKEN

Chicken Broccoli Salad With Almond Dressing

Preparation Time: 5 minutes
Cooking Time: 40 minutes
Servings: 6
Ingredients:

- 2 chicken breasts

- 1 pound broccoli, cut into florets

- 1 Almond, peeled and pitted

- ½ lemon, juiced

- 2 garlic cloves

- ¼ teaspoon chili powder

- ¼ teaspoon minutes powder

Directions:

1. Cook the chicken in a large pot of salty water.

2. Drain and cut the chicken into small cubes. Place in a salad bowl.

3. Add the broccoli and mix well.

4. Combine the Almond, lemon juice, garlic, chili powder, minutes powder, salt, and pepper in a blender. Pulse until smooth. Spoon over the salad with the dressing and blend well. Serve the salad fresh.

Nutrition:

- Calories: 195,
- Fats: 11g,
- Proteins: 14g,
- Carbohydrates: 3g

Herbed Roasted Chicken Breasts

Preparation Time: 5 minutes
Cooking Time: 50 minutes
Servings: 4
Ingredients:

- 2 tablespoons extra virgin olive oil

- 2 tablespoons chopped parsley

- 2 tablespoons chopped cilantro

- 1 teaspoon dried oregano

- 1 teaspoon dried basil

- 2 tablespoons lemon juice

- 4 chicken breasts

Directions:

1. Combine the oil, parsley, cilantro, oregano, basil, lemon juice, salt, and pepper in a bowl.

2. Spread this mixture over the chicken and rub it well into the meat. Place in a deep dish baking pan and cover with aluminum foil.

3. Cook in the preheated oven at 350°F for 20 minutes, then remove the foil and cook for 25 additional minutes. Serve the chicken warm and fresh with your favorite side dish.

Nutrition:
- Calories: 330,
- Fats: 15g,
- Proteins: 40.7g,
- Carbohydrates: 1g

Marinated Chicken Breasts

Preparation Time: 5 minutes
Cooking Time: 2 hours
Servings: 4
Ingredients:

- 4 chicken breasts

- Salt and pepper to taste

- 1 lemon, juiced

- 1 rosemary sprig

- 1 thyme sprig

- 2 garlic cloves, crushed

- 2 sage leaves

- 3 tablespoons extra virgin olive oil

- ½ cup buttermilk

Directions:

1. Boil the chicken with salt and pepper and place it in a resealable bag.

2. Add remaining ingredients and seal bag.

3. Refrigerate for at least 1 hour.

4. After 1 hour, heat a roasting pan over medium heat, then place the chicken on the grill.

5. Cook on each side for 8–10 minutes or until juices are gone.

6. Serve the chicken warm with your favorite side dish.

Nutrition:

- Calories: 371,
- Fats: 21g,
- Proteins: 46g,
- Carbohydrates: 2g

Creamy Penne

Preparation Time: 10 minutes
Cooking Time: 25 minutes
Servings: 4
Ingredients:

- ½ cup penne, dried
- 9 oz. chicken fillet
- 1 teaspoon Italian seasoning
- 1 tablespoon olive oil
- 1 tomato, chopped
- 1 cup heavy cream
- 1 tablespoon fresh basil, chopped
- ½ teaspoon salt
- 2 oz. Parmesan, grated
- 1 cup water for cooking

Directions:

1. Pour water into the pan, add penne, and boil it for 15 minutes. Then drain water.
2. In a pan, add in the olive oil and heat it up.
3. Slice the chicken fillet and put it in the hot oil.
4. Sprinkle chicken with Italian seasoning and roast for 2 minutes from each side.
5. Then add fresh basil, salt, tomato, and grated cheese.
6. Stir well.

7. Add heavy cream and cooked penne.

8. Cook the meat for 5 minutes more over medium heat. Stir it from time to time.

Nutrition:
- Calories: 388,
- Fats: 23.4g,
- Proteins: 17.6g,
- Carbohydrates: 17.6g,
- Fibers: 0.2g

Garlic Chicken Balls

Preparation Time: 15 minutes
Cooking Time: 10 minutes
Servings: 4
Ingredients:

- 2 cups ground chicken
- 1 teaspoon minced garlic
- 1 teaspoon dried dill
- 1/3 carrot, grated
- 1 egg, beaten
- 1 tablespoon olive oil
- ¼ cup coconut flakes
- ½ teaspoon salt

Directions:

1. In the mixing bowl, mix up ground chicken, minced garlic, dried dill, carrot, egg, and salt.

2. Stir the chicken mixture with the help of the fingertips until homogenous.

3. Then make medium balls from the mixture.

4. Coat every chicken ball in coconut flakes.

5. Heat up olive oil in the skillet.

6. Add chicken balls and cook them for 3 minutes from each side. The cooked chicken balls will have a golden-brown color.

Nutrition:

- Calories: 200,
- Fats: 11.5g,
- Proteins: 21.9g,
- Carbohydrates: 1.7g,

Chicken Enchilada Rollups

Preparation Time: 10 minutes
Cooking Time: 40 minutes
Servings: 4
1 Leaner, 3 Green, 1 fat, 1.5 Condiments
Ingredients:

- 4 boneless, skinless chicken breasts (24-oz total)

- 1 teaspoon minutes

- 1 minced garlic clove

- 1 teaspoon oregano

- 1/2 cup diced tomatoes

- 2 teaspoons chili powder

- 1 (10-oz) can mild enchilada sauce

- 3/4 cup low-fat shredded blue cheese

- 2 1/2 cups cauliflower, grated

- 2 green onions, chopped

- 1 tablespoon of water

- 1/8 teaspoon cayenne

Directions:

1. Preheat the oven to 375° F.

2. Combine the oregano, cumin, garlic, and chili powder in a bowl. Rub the mixture on each chicken.

3. Lightly spray a baking dish and pour a thin layer of the enchilada sauce on the bottom of the dish.

4. Lay the chicken, cut-side up on a cutting board. Top each center of the chicken with tomatoes, cayenne, and cheese. Roll each chicken up and set them seam side down in the dish.

5. Using foil to cover, bake for 30 minutes.

6. Remove foil after 30 minutes and bake for another 12 minutes or until the chicken is cooked through.

7. While the rollups are baking, add the cauliflower and water in a microwave and microwave for 5 minutes or until tender.

8. Serve the roll-ups alone or enjoy them over the cauliflower.

Nutrition:
- Calories: 450;
- Protein: 46.8g;
- Fat: 23g;
- Carbs: 12.4g

SOUP

White Bean and Cabbage Soup

Preparation Time: 5 minutes
Cooking Time: 30 minutes
Servings: 4
Ingredients:

- 1 tablespoon of olive oil

- 4 chopped carrots

- 4 chopped stalks of celery or 1 chopped bok choy

- 1 chopped onion

- 2 cloves of minced garlic

- 1 chopped cabbage head

- ½ lb. of northern beans soaked in water overnight (drained)

- 6 cups of chicken broth

- 3 cups of water

Directions:

1. Sauté vegetables in oil.

2. Add the rest of the ingredients and cook for 30 minutes on medium-low heat.

Nutrition:

- Calories: 423;
- Fat: 2 g;
- Fiber: 0 g;
- Carbs: 20 g;
- Protein: 33 g

Flavorful Broccoli Soup

Preparation Time: 10 minutes
Cooking Time: 4 hours 15 minutes
Servings: 6
Ingredients:

- 20 oz. broccoli florets

- 4 oz. cream cheese

- 8 oz. Cheddar cheese; shredded

- 1/2 tsp. paprika

- 1/2 tsp. ground mustard

- 3 cups chicken stock

- 2 garlic cloves; chopped

- 1 onion; diced

- 1 cup carrots; shredded

- 1/4 tsp. baking soda

- 1/4 tsp. salt

Directions:

1. To a Crock-Pot, add all of the ingredients except cream cheese and Cheddar cheese and mix well.

2. Cover and cook on low for 4 hours.

3. Purée the soup using an immersion blender until it's smooth.

4. Stir in the cream cheese and Cheddar cheese.

5. Cover and cook on low for 15 minutes more.

6. Season with pepper and salt.

7. Serve and enjoy.

Nutrition:
- Calories 275;
- Fat 19 g;
- Carbohydrates 19 g;
- Sugar 4 g;
- Protein 14 g;
- Cholesterol 60 mg

Lentil Soup

Preparation Time: 10 minutes
Cooking Time: 2 hours
Servings: 4
Ingredients:

- 2 tablespoons olive oil
- 2 chopped onions
- 1 chopped red pepper
- 1 chopped carrot
- 2 minced garlic cloves
- ½ teaspoon minutes
- ¾ teaspoon thyme
- 1 bay leaf
- 8 cups chicken broth
- 2 chopped tomatoes
- ½ pound dried lentils (1¼ cup)
- Optional: add bacon or ham to flavor.
- 1 teaspoon salt
- ¼ teaspoon pepper
- Handful spinach

Directions:

1. Sauté vegetables in oil.

2. Combine all the ingredients and (except spinach and spices). Cover and cook for 2 hours under low pressure.

3. Spinach and spices are added.

Nutrition:

- Calories: 257;
- Fat: 13 g;
- Fiber: 37 g;
- Carbs: 11g
- Protein: 8 g

Black Bean Soup

Preparation Time: 5 minutes

Cooking Time: 1 hour

Servings: 4

Ingredients:

- 1 pound of dry black beans (soak in water overnight and drain water)
- 1 tablespoon of olive oil
- 2 cups of chopped onion or 1 leek
- 1 cup of chopped carrots
- 4 cloves of minced garlic
- 2 teaspoons of minutes
- ¼ teaspoon of red pepper flakes
- 4 cups of chicken broth
- 4 cups of water
- ¼ teaspoon of thyme
- 2 chopped tomatoes or 1 (14 oz.) can of tomatoes
- 1½ teaspoon of salt
- Optional: add bacon or ham to flavor.
- Chopped green onions to garnish

Directions:

Sauté vegetables in oil. Add all of the ingredients and cook on the stovetop on medium-low. Heat for 1 hour.

Nutrition:

- Calories: 508;
- Fat: 12 g;
- Fiber: 9 g;
- Carbs: 24 g;
- Protein: 40 g

Homemade Vegetable Broth

Preparation Time: 5 minutes
Cooking Time: 30 minutes
Servings: 4
Ingredients:

- 1 tablespoon olive oil
- 1 chopped onion
- 2 chopped stalks celery
- 2 chopped carrots
- 1 head bok choy
- 6 cups or 1 package of fresh spinach
- 2 ¼ water
- 1 tablespoon salt
- ½ teaspoon pepper
- 1 teaspoon fresh sage

Directions:

1. Sauté vegetables in oil. Add water and simmer for 1 hour.

2. Keep adding water as required.

3. Pour broth mixture into pint and quart mason jars.

4. Leave one full inch of space from the top of the jar, or it will crack when it freezes, and liquid expands. Jars can stay in the freezer for up to a year.

5. Take out and use whenever you make a soup.

Nutrition:

- Calories: 140;
- Fat: 2 g;
- Fiber: 23 g;
- Carbs: 22 g;
- Protein: 47 g

Tasty Basil Tomato Soup

Preparation Time: 10 minutes
Cooking Time: 6 hours
Servings: 6
Ingredients:

- 28 oz. of can whole peeled tomatoes
- 1/2 cup of fresh basil leaves
- 4 cups of chicken stock
- 1 tsp. of red pepper flakes
- 3 garlic cloves; peeled
- 2 onions; diced
- 3 carrots; peeled and diced
- 3 tbsps. of olive oil
- 1 tsp. of salt

Directions:

1. For a Crock-Pot, add all the ingredients and mix well.

2. Cover and cook on low for 6 hours.

3. Purée the soup until smooth, using an immersion blender.

4. Season soup with pepper and salt.

5. Serve and enjoy.

Nutrition:

- Calories 126;
- Fat 5 g;
- Carbohydrates 13 g;
- Sugar 7 g;
- Protein 5 g;
- Cholesterol 0 mg

Mixed Vegetable Soup

Preparation Time: 5 minutes
Cooking Time: 30 minutes
Servings: 4
Ingredients:

- 1 chopped leek and 1 chopped bok choy

- 4 chopped carrots

- 2 cloves of minced garlic

- 1 chopped zucchini

- 2 chopped tomatoes

- 1 cup of garbanzo beans soaked in water overnight (drained)

- 5 chopped potatoes

- 8 cups of broth

- 1 teaspoon of basil

- ½ cup of amaranth

Directions:

1. Sauté the first four ingredients, adding garlic at the last minute.

2. Add the rest of the ingredients and simmer on the stove for 25 minutes.

Nutrition:

- Calories: 241;
- Fat: 2 g;
- Carbs: 9 g;
- Protein: 22 g

SALAD

Potato Tuna Salad

Preparation Time: 4 hours and 20 minutes
Cooking Time: 10 minutes
Servings: 1
Ingredients:

- 1 potato, peeled and sliced into cubes

- 1/12 cup plain yogurt

- 1/12 cup mayonnaise

- 1/6 garlic clove, crushed and minced

- 1/6 tablespoon almond milk

- 1/6 tablespoon fresh dill, chopped

- ½ teaspoon lemon zest

- Salt to taste

- 1 cup cucumber, chopped

- ¼ cup scallions, chopped

- ¼ cup radishes, chopped

- (9 oz) canned tuna flakes

- 1/2 hard-boiled eggs, chopped

- 1 cups lettuce, chopped

Directions:
1. Fill your pot with water.
2. Add the potatoes and boil.
3. Cook for 15 minutes or till slightly tender.
4. Drain and let cool.

5. In a bowl, mix the yogurt, mayo, garlic, almond milk, fresh dill, lemon zest, and salt.
6. Stir in the potatoes, tuna flakes, and eggs.
7. Mix well.
8. Chill in the refrigerator for 4 hours.
9. Stir in the shredded lettuce before serving.

Nutrition:
- Calories: 243;
- Fat: 9.9g;
- Saturated fat: 2g;
- Carbohydrates: 22.2g;
- Fiber: 4.6g;
- Protein: 17.5g

High Protein Salad

Preparation Time: 5 minutes
Cooking Time: 5 minutes
Servings: 1
Ingredients:
Salad:

- 1(15 oz) can green kidney beans

- 1/4 tablespoon capers

- 1/4 handfuls arugula

- 1(15 oz) can of lentils

Dressing:

- 1/1 tablespoon caper brine

- 1/1 tablespoon tamari

- 1/1 tablespoon balsamic vinegar

- 2/2 tablespoon peanut butter

- 2/2 tablespoon hot sauce

- 2/1 tablespoon tahini

Directions:
For the dressing:
1. In a bowl, stir all the ingredients until they come together to form a smooth dressing.

For the salad:
2. Mix the beans, arugula, capers, and lentils. Top with the dressing and serve.

Nutrition:
- Calories: 205;

- Fat: 2g;
- Protein: 13g;
- Carbs: 31g;
- Fiber: 17g

Rice and Veggie Bowl

Preparation Time: 5 minutes
Cooking Time: 15 minutes
Servings: 1
Ingredients:

- 1/3 tablespoon coconut oil

- 1/2 teaspoon ground minutes

- 1/2 teaspoon ground turmeric

- 1/3 teaspoon chili powder

- 1 red bell pepper, chopped

- 1/2 tablespoon tomato paste

- 1 bunch of broccoli, cut into bite-sized-florets with short stems 1/2 teaspoon salt, to taste

- 1 large red onion, sliced

- 1/2 garlic clove, minced

- 1/2 head of cauliflower, sliced into bite-sized florets 1/2 cups cooked rice

- Newly ground black pepper to taste

Directions:

1. Start with Warminster up the coconut oil over medium-high heat.
2. Stir in the turmeric, minutes, chili powder, salt, and tomato paste.
3. Cook the content for 1 minute. Stir repeatedly until the spices are fragrant.
4. Add the garlic and onion. Fry for 2,5 to 3,3 minutes until the onions are softened.

5. Add the broccoli, cauliflower, and bell pepper. Cover, then cook for 3 to 4 minutes and stir occasionally.
6. Add the cooked rice. Stir so it will combine well with the vegetables. Cook for 2 to 3 minutes. Stir until the rice Is warm.
7. Check the seasoning and change to taste if desired.
8. Lessen the heat and cook on low for 2 to 3 more minutes so the flavors will meld.
9. Serve with freshly ground black pepper.

Nutrition:
- Calories: 260;
- Fat: 9g;
- Protein: 9g;
- Carbs: 36g;
- Fiber: 5g

Squash Black Bean Bowl

Preparation Time: 5 minutes
Cooking Time: 30 minutes
Servings: 1
Ingredients:

- 1 large spaghetti squash, halved,

- 1/3 cup water (or 2 tablespoon olive oil, rubbed on the inside of squash)

Black bean filling:

- 1/2 (15 oz) can of black beans, emptied and rinsed 1/2 cup fire-roasted corn (or frozen sweet corn) 1/2 cup thinly sliced red cabbage

- 1/2 tablespoon chopped green onion, green and white parts ¼ cup chopped fresh coriander

- ½ lime, juiced or to taste

- Pepper and salt, to taste

Avocado mash:

- One ripe avocado, mashed

- ½ lime, juiced or to taste

- ¼ teaspoon minutes

- Pepper and pinch of sea salt

Directions:

1. Preheat the oven to 400°F.
2. Chop the squash in part and scoop out the seeds with a spoon, like a pumpkin.

3. Fill the roasting pan with 1/3 cup of water. Lay the squash, cut side down, in the pan. Bake for 30 minutes until soft and tender.
4. While this is baking, mix all the ingredients for the black bean filling in a medium-sized bowl.
5. In a small dish, crush the avocado and blend in the avocado mash ingredients.
6. Eliminutesate the squash from the oven and let it cool for 5 minutes. Scrape the squash with a fork so that it looks like spaghetti noodles. Then, fill it with black bean filling and top with avocado mash.
7. Serve and enjoy.

Nutrition:
- Calories: 85;
- Fat: 0.5g;
- Protein: 4g;
- Carbs: 6g;
- Fiber: 4g

Pea Salad

Preparation Time: 40 minutes
Cooking Time: 0 minutes
Servings: 1
Ingredients:

- 1/2 cup chickpeas, rinsed and drained

- 1/2 cups peas, divided

- 1 tablespoon olive oil

- ½ cup buttermilk

- 2 cups pea greens

- 1/2 carrots shaved

- 1/4 cup snow peas, trimmed

Directions:

1. Add the chickpeas and half of the peas to your food processor.
2. Season with salt.
3. Pulse until smooth. Set aside.
4. In a bowl, toss the remaining peas in oil, milk, salt, and pepper.
5. Transfer the mixture to your food processor.
6. Process until pureed.
7. Transfer this mixture to a bowl.
8. Arrange the pea greens on a serving plate.
9. Top with the shaved carrots and snow peas.
10. Stir in the pea and milk dressing. Serve with the reserved chickpea hummus.

Nutrition:

- Calories: 214;
- Fat: 8.6g;
- Carbohydrates: 27.3g;
- Protein: 8g

Snap Pea Salad

Preparation Time: 1 hour
Cooking Time: 0 minutes
Servings: 1
Ingredients:

- 1/2 tablespoons mayonnaise

- ¾ teaspoon celery seed

- ¼ cup cider vinegar

- 1/2 teaspoon yellow mustard

- 1/2 tablespoon sugar

- Salt and pepper to taste

- 1 oz. radishes, sliced thinly

- 2 oz. sugar snap peas, sliced thinly

Directions:

1. In a bowl, combine the mayonnaise, celery seeds, vinegar, mustard, sugar, salt, and pepper.
2. Stir in the radishes and snap peas.
3. Refrigerate for 30 minutes.

Nutrition:

- Calories: 69;
- Fat: 3.7g;
- Saturated fat: 0.6g;
- Carbohydrates: 7.1g;
- Fiber: 1.8g;
- Protein: 2g

Cucumber Tomato Chopped Salad

Preparation Time: 15 minutes
Cooking Time: 0 minutes
Servings: 1
Ingredients:

- 1/4 cup light mayonnaise

- 1/2 tablespoon lemon juice

- 1/2 tablespoon fresh dill, chopped

- 1/2 tablespoon chive, chopped

- 1/4 cup feta cheese, crumbled

- 1/2 red onion, chopped

- 1/2 cucumber, diced

- 1/2 radish, diced

- 1 tomato, diced

- Chives, chopped

Directions:

1. Combine the mayonnaise, lemon juice, fresh dill, chives, feta cheese, salt, and pepper in a bowl.
2. Mix well.
3. Stir in the onion, cucumber, radish, and tomatoes.
4. Coat evenly.
5. Garnish with the chopped chives.

Nutrition:

- Calories: 187;
- Fat: 16.7g;
- Carbohydrates: 6.7g;
- Protein: 3.3g

Zucchini Pasta Salad

Preparation Time: 4 minutes
Cooking Time: 0 minutes
Servings: 1
Ingredients:

- 1 tablespoon olive oil

- 1/2 teaspoons dijon mustard

- 1/3 tablespoons red-wine vinegar

- 1/2 garlic clove, grated

- 2 tablespoons fresh oregano, chopped

- 1/2 shallot, chopped

- ¼ teaspoon red pepper flakes

- 4 oz. zucchini noodles

- ¼ cup Kalamata olives pitted

- 1 cups cherry tomato, sliced in half

- ¾ cup parmesan cheese shaved

Directions:

1. Mix the olive oil, Dijon mustard, red wine vinegar, garlic, oregano, shallot, and red pepper flakes in a bowl.
2. Stir in the zucchini noodles.
3. Sprinkle on top the olives, tomatoes, and Parmesan cheese.

Nutrition:

- Calories: 299;
- Fat: 24.7g;
- Carbohydrates: 11.6g;
- Protein: 7g

Wasabi Tuna Asian Salad

Preparation Time: 30 minutes
Cooking Time: 10 minutes
Servings: 1
1 Leaner, 3 Green, 1 fat, 1.5 Condiments
Ingredients:
- 1 teaspoon Lime juice
- Non-stick cooking spray
- Pepper/dash of salt
- 1 teaspoon Wasabi paste
- 1/2 cup Chopped or shredded cucumbers
- 1 cup Bok Choy stalks
- 8 oz. Raw tuna steak

Directions:
Fish:
1. Preheat your skillet to medium heat. Mix your wasabi and lime juice; coat the tuna steaks.
2. Use a non-stick cooking spray on your skillet for 10 seconds.
3. Put your tuna steaks on the skillet and cook over medium heat until you get the desired doneness.

Salad:
1. Slice the cucumber into match-stick tiny sizes.
2. Cut the bok Choy into minute pieces.
3. Toss gently with pepper, salt, and olive oil if you want.
4. Enjoy your food.

Nutrition:
- Protein: 61g;
- Cholesterol: 115mg;
- Saturated fats: 2g;
- Calories: 380

DESSERT

Vanilla Chocolate Cheesecake

Preparation Time: 10 minutes
Cooking Time: 60 minutes
Servings: 1
1 Fueling, 1 Fat, 1/2 Lean, 3 Condiments
Ingredients:

- 4 tablespoons cold water

- 2 sachets Optavia Essential Double Chocolate Brownie

- 1/2 tablespoon unsalted butter, melted

- 1 cup reduced-fat plain Greek yogurt

- 3 tablespoons light cream cheese

- 1 egg

- 2 teaspoons stevia

- 1/2 teaspoon pumpkin pie spice

- 1 teaspoon pure vanilla extract

- 1/8 teaspoon salt

- 1/2 teaspoon ground cinnamon

Directions:

1. Preheat your oven to 350° F.

2. Add the chocolate brownie, butter, and water to a bowl and mix well to combine.

3. Divide the mixture among two lightly greased mini springform pans. To shape thin crusts, press the mixture into the pan's bottom and then bake for 15 minutes.

4. While baking, add the remaining ingredients to a medium bowl and mix until well combined, and then divide among the two pans.

5. Lower oven temperature to 300° F. Bake for another 35 minutes or until the edges of the cheesecake turn golden brown and a toothpick inserted into the center comes out clean.

6. Remove from the oven. Leave to cool for a few minutes before cutting and slicing.

7. Enjoy!

Nutrition:
- Calories: 316;
- Fat: 25g;
- Protein: 21g;
- Carbs: 16g.

CONCLUSION

The Lean and Green Meal regimen's primary goal is to help people reduce weight and obesity through a controlled portion of meals and snacks. The meals are lower in calories and carbohydrates and higher in protein to encourage weight loss. It offers a relatively balanced diet as the meals call for consuming all food classes in reasonable proportions.

For most people, it is challenging to alter eating habits drastically. It is advisable to gradually find fun ways to incorporate the Lean and Green meals into your regular diet. The recipes in this cookbook are delicious and exciting and shouldn't be challenging to integrate. Also, it is not advisable to suddenly stop the regimen; you are likely to regain the weight.

Air-frying the food can make the meals easier to incorporate. The cooking time is cut in half, and oil usage is minimized, making the food more nutritious. This is beneficial since it helps you eat less of those foods that are not so healthy and change your diet. This way, people can lose weight through a healthy way of eating food.

Another important thing that people need to know when it comes to the Lean and Green Meals is that you do not have to starve yourself even though it is a calorie-restricted regimen. It does not mean that you cannot eat food that you like. It only means that you will have to be picky about the food that you eat. Lean and Green Meals allows people to live a healthy lifestyle using food as their fuel and not as their enemy.

In a nutshell, Lean and Green Meal is intended to be practiced and is specifically structured to help people lose weight. It is not just another weight loss program; it's a lifestyle change that helps people shed pounds and maintain good health.

Now that you are at the end of this book, I know you are more than inspired to have healthier choices and have a more wonderful life.

THE
COMPLETE

LEAN &
GREEN
diet cookbook

**Make Your Weight Loss
Easier and More
Sustainable**

KULTURE KITCHEN